Uncovering and Recognising
Awareness

Uncovering and Recognising
Awareness

Wasyl Nimenko

Goalpath Books

Published by Goalpath Books 2024

Uncovering and Recognising Awareness

ISBN 978-1-908142-72-6

Wasyl Nimenko was born in Ipswich, England. His mother was from Tubbercurry in the west of Ireland, his father from Dnipropetrovsk (now Dnipro) in central Ukraine. After studying medicine in London from 1974-1979, he began training and working as a psychiatrist. He worked at the 2,200 bed St Bernard's Hospital *(previously known as the 'Hanwell Insane Asylum' and the 'Hanwell Pauper and Lunatic Asylum')* but left psychiatry because of the overemphasis on the chemical causes and treatments of mental health problems.

He left psychiatry to train as a GP and a psychotherapist. From 1982 - 1991 he worked with survivors of torture. He worked independently, in the NHS, with the homeless and also with the emergency services and the armed forces.

In 1984 Wasyl Nimenko researched the stress of using virtual reality for Xerox among the first users of the Xerox Star, technology which has since become the standard in personal computers. In 2011 he carried out research into the use of archaeology in the psychological decompression of wounded soldiers, a service which is now available internationally to the armed forces as 'Operation Nightingale.' In 2013 he researched Post Repatriation Stress Disorder which was first described in 2015.

Although Wasyl Nimenko's professional activities have chiefly been in the UK he has also lived and worked in India, New Zealand and Australia. At present his main interest is in uncovering, recognising and realising our natural happiness.

ALSO BY WASYL NIMENKO

Non-Fiction

Einstein and Ramana Maharshi
Removing Our Delusion of Separateness
Do you need a Doctor, Therapist or Guru?
Acceptance and Meaning in Grief
Carl Jung and Ramana Maharshi
Notes from the Inside
The Spiritual Nature of Addictions

Fiction

Invisible Bullets

Travel

Searching in Secret India
Searching in Secret New Zealand and Australia
Searching in Secret Orkney

Poems

The Fool's Poems Part I
The Fool's Poems Part II

CONTENTS

Introduction

1. Awareness   1

2. Mind   42

3. What we cannot see   57

4. Unifying separateness   67

5. Inside help   76

6. Importance   89

    Index   114

Introduction

We have our own unique way to realise who we are, what our purpose is and how to find happiness. The question of 'Who we are inside' or 'Who am I' does not seem important to those who appear to have found happiness in the external world. Because they feel happy, they have no interest in searching further.

The question of 'who am I' usually only comes to those who have suffered and who know the answer to finding happiness is somewhere inside.

In trying to answer this question of 'who am I,' first we have to ask and find out 'what we are not.' Eventually we see 'what we are not' is simply *our thoughts, our ego.*

With determined questioning of 'Who' is asking, we may uncover and recognise ourself without thoughts, and see only one thing is left . . . our awareness of our true Self.

Blissful though this may be for a time, this state of awareness is only a temporary glimpse because *our thoughts, our ego* does not give up trying to hide the true inner Self we have seen and are now intermittently aware of.

With continuing effort, uncovering who we are becomes present more of the time during our daily living. The experience of time without thoughts, of just awareness of being, becomes more frequent.

The notes here are from the practical experiences we may have while uncovering, recognising and realising who we are.

1.

Awareness

Not the I, who I think I am

The true intention of the question, What is the meaning of life? is Who am I? or you may prefer, What am I? You know this because something else inside is asking the question, so you are not just these almost ceaseless thoughts.

You can ask where does this I come from? Turning inwards further, you can only ask, Who is asking this? The who which is asking seems to have always been here, the most aware part of what I am.

Only then, I realise there is a permanent awareness, a witness who was here before I could think, and who will always be here.

Then, I realise the thinking process, which serves the body, is ceaselessly trying to cover up and prevent the witness from being known.

1

The question

Few of us ask the question Who am I? Why would you? You would only ask if you are unhappy, unhappy with how you are, unhappy with your thoughts.

It is a question which opens a door, to find meaning in living in relation to everything around us and to what we cannot see.

Witness

I sit and ask Who am I? Then find I have to ask Who is asking this? It is the witness who is asking.

I ask Who or What is this witness? The witness is awareness. The witness is awareness of I am.

It witnessed everything I have been or done since existing, so where did it come from or enter me from, where will it go? We do not know.

Is the witness more than awareness? Is awareness the consciousness of the universe? Is this the most serious mystery but also a blessing?

Repeatedly distracted by intellectual thoughts of what it is, I lose the awareness but the witness knows this, and I am again aware I am the witness.

I am aware I am, therefore, I think

What a simple profound error to persist in believing 'I think therefore I am,' because, you have to have Awareness of existence or I am-ness before you can have the thought of it.

You cannot have the thought of your existence or I am-ness before being aware of your existence or I am-ness. You have to have the experience of being I am-ness before you can think about it.

To believe 'I think therefore I am' misplaces thinking before and above awareness, because thinking is a servant of awareness. Awareness illuminates the working of your mind.

Awareness lights you up when your mind is awake, when it is simply asleep or when it is dreaming. It is present all the time, always . . . permanent.

Thinking cannot understand awareness. It can only accept not being able to find words for awareness, but awareness is the witness of thinking, aware of I am-ness is our highest state.

Being the presence of awareness

Seeking the answer to 'Who am I' at first and repeatedly is a journey of exclusion. When all possibilities are gone there is only the presence.

The presence is the awareness of I am, the presence of I am needs no I because what is left is Am-ness.

Awareness and consciousness

Consciousness is broad, open to attend to streams of thought.
Awareness is focused, concentrating attention on one thought.

Consciousness can be discussed and categorised.
Awareness is subjective, transcendent and beyond words.

Method

The experience of realising the 'Self' has no description.
The only useful help is describing what it is not.
Although universal, each of us must uncover it on our own.

It begins with asking 'Who am I' and in asking, discovering
what 'I' am not, i.e. thoughts, or the body, until eventually we
ask 'Who is asking this.'

Who is asking is witnessing everything in our life. We know
the witness has been here since our first memory, so the
witness is us.

We then ask if it is not thoughts, 'What is this witness?' We can
then only ask 'What is before thoughts,' which can only be our
Awareness.

We then ask, 'Who or what is this Awareness?'
The Awareness is being aware that I Am, or I Am-ness.
I am the witness which is awareness of being.

Getting rid of unhelpful words there is only the Awareness.
With no words and no thoughts, I am still.
In this stillness I am.

The witness

What is this I the witness? Where did it come from? Is the witness some kind of energy, life itself, or something greater like the stuff of the universe, the stuff being awareness of consciousness.

Is this awareness our essence, our spirit? Does it carry on in a new form or without form when we die? Does it return to part of something greater? It has to go somewhere as it cannot go nowhere.

Animals are conscious too and have the same awareness. Perhaps they are freer, unburdened by our language, less sophisticated, more natural in relating their oneness, perhaps more intelligent.

I Am-ness

In answering 'Who am I' You become aware of the witness. The witness has seen and been through everything with you, but is unchanged.

In asking who this witness is, the witness is awareness.
In asking 'What is this awareness of' it is awareness of I am.

Staying with just being aware of I am-ness is what I am.
When all else is stripped away, and all the veils are removed, awareness of I am-ness is the sereneness of impersonal being, identical to sat-chit-ananda, being-conscious-bliss.

Aware of being

The witness is awareness.
The witness is awareness of existence, of being, of I am.
The witness is awareness - the same as all awareness.

Unveiling

In asking 'Who am I' we realise who we are by intermittent glimpses of awareness.

Because thinking veils awareness, effort is needed to stop thinking's veiling.

Veils of Ignorance

Identifying with thoughts covers up the Self which creates the delusion 'I am my thinking.'

Oneness of being

It seems the closest to a single word for Experiencing awareness of being, is the triplet, Being-Consciousness-Bliss, Sat-Chit-Ananada, but this can be simplified and can be more clearly understood.

In asking 'Who am I,' we realise there is a witness. In asking 'Who is the witness' we realise it is Awareness. In asking 'Who is the awareness of' we realise it is I am-ness. In asking 'Who is this I am-ness' we realise I amness is bigger.

In asking is there an individual I separate from everything, we realise there is only 'I am' and everything is of the same nature. If you can identify with and call Everything That, you can say I am That or That I am.

'Awareness of I am That' is oneness of being, It is a relief realising what we are, and it is also bliss. Aware I am That amness can be a single word, Awareiamthat.

Awareiamthat is simple.
Awareiamthat has a single unified Who.
Awareiamthat is one entity of which we are part.
Awareiamthat is what I am, is You, is Everything.

The witness is the Self

The witness is awareness – the ego is thoughts
Awareness is still -the ego restlessly thinks
Awareness listens - the ego speaks
Awareness is serene - the ego seeks identity and satisfaction
Awareness is veiled by thoughts - the ego creates thoughts
Awareness unifies knowledge and knower - the ego separates.

One is part of the other

The witness is awareness, like a still and serene light
Awareness lets thoughts be seen as the ego so that the body can
function. So, are thoughts who we are?

Thoughts exist only because of the light of awareness, but the
ego tries to conceal the light of awareness. Thoughts create a
fight, in which the witness is veiled.

Effort our most effective weapon

Seeking importance, thoughts appear, masquerading as a separate entity, the ego. Only with your effort can you unveil the witness, your awareness, the Self. Then ignorance can be removed.

Self and non-Self

The ego uses every opportunity to create thoughts, creating the illusion that it is you.

Asking 'Who am I?' with extinction of the personal I, you become aware of glimpses, unveiling the true Self.

The witness is awareness, thought-free in serene stillness. It is nothing else and also everything else.

The natural rhythm of Who am I?

After the witness is identified and recognised as awareness
Peace and bliss are experienced.
Then, sitting still with closed eyes, without warning,
A thought intrudes.
Who noticed this thought has intruded?
The witness noticed it.
Who is the witness?
The witness is awareness.

After the witness is identified and recognised as awareness
Peace and bliss are experienced.
Then, sitting still with closed eyes, without warning,
Another thought intrudes.
Who noticed this thought has intruded?
The witness noticed it.
Who is the witness?
The witness is awareness.

After the witness is identified and recognised as awareness
Peace and bliss are experienced.
Then, sitting still with closed eyes, without warning,
Another thought intrudes.
Who noticed this thought has intruded?
The witness noticed it.
Who is the witness?
The witness is awareness.

The nature and place of the mind and body

Awareness is not in the mind or of the mind, the mind is of it because the mind can only function because of the existence of awareness.

Awareness is not in the body or of the body, the body is of it because the body can only function because of the existence of awareness.

Hearing, sight, touch, taste and smell alert us to our surroundings. The kidneys and liver clean our blood, whilst the lungs exchange gases for the heart to deliver to the brain so the mind can processes information for the best explanation.

Just as the mind is aware of and processes information from all the organs, the witness is aware of the totality of the mind and body. The witness is the highest level of what we are. It is what we identify with and recognise as our Self.

Without a name

The ego tries to be important all the time, and has success most of the time, but just sometime we have a glimpse when we know this.

As we see more of what we are, slowly and gently these glimpses grow. It becomes easier to stay on the path we always knew was here.

Although awareness, discernment and sensitivity to subtle distractions when supported by simplicity and discipline seem enough, we still seem to need almost endless reminding just to stay on the path of awareness.

Being and knowing

Words cannot let anything subjective be experienced. I can tell you about riding a bicycle but you cannot experience it without riding. Likewise, if I tell you about awareness of I Am-ness, you may now believe it exists but the only way to experience I Am-ness is to find it and be it.

Staring

If from behind my closed eyelids, thoughts do not interrupt this awareness, I am happy being awareness.

Each day brings its worldly, basic needs. Each day brings responsibilities. Each day we look for relief from suffering and avoidance of pain.

It all has one purpose, to be able to stare happy into full emptiness, experiencing the bliss of just being awareness.

Levels of attainment

Accepting we are not the body or its thoughts, the first experience is a waking up of awareness. Then, trying to have no thoughts other than awareness only, you repeatedly get interruptions by thoughts.

Seeing and accepting a background awareness of stillness which although veiled is permanent, you see thoughts come and go like temporary passing clouds. Then you realise they fight to always be present first.

Even with more effort, thoughts ceaselessly interrupt stillness. Then with repeated witnessing the nature of thoughts, awareness sees thought as a need of the body's existence.

What is unveiled is that thoughts have a mundane function to support the body and mind so the Self can be unveiled and realised.

The fight shows awareness as stillness which is peace, and thoughts as a disturbance. But then when you are busy doing things, there is a gentleness of the witness unveiled as awareness, as the answer to 'Who am I.'

The perfection of imperfection

Perfection is repeatedly being distracted, veering off the path, then getting back up, continuing to be on the path.

Perfection is repeatedly recovering from being distracted cherishing and not letting go of the certainty of awareness of I am-ness, no matter what tries to eclipse this.

Attend to the purpose for which you have come

Remember that eventually you must confront your death, so attend now to what you have come here for.

We can only accomplish what we have come here for if we are in our most aware state.

Remember to be still many times a day, so remember now to stand still many times a day.

Make effort to be in your most aware state; stillness.

Remember to be still many times a day, so remember now to let thoughts be still many times a day.

Make effort to just be still.

Remember all the time to just be still, so remember now to remember to just be still.

Reclaiming

When the witness, the awareness of I am-ness is uncovered and experienced, ask 'Who' uncovered the witness.

Each time we notice thoughts have crept in and intruded, ask 'Who' has noticed thoughts have crept in.

With loss of awareness of I am-ness, ask 'Who' has noticed this loss of awareness.

Continual to continuous

At first, when we recover our true awareness we want to keep it but we notice thoughts continually intrude and overpower it.

Thoughts creep in and intrude continually, but thoughts can be overcome by continually trying to make awareness continuous.

Who am I?

Who is the witness? Who is asking this?
The witness is the awareness not just of seeing everything but
of a greater understanding than this limited thinking brain.

The witness is the awareness of being
The witness is aware of I am
The witness is not just aware of I am
But also aware of I am more than I am.

It is aware I am not just part of a more extensive awareness
It is aware I am the same as the more extensive awareness
It is aware I am one and the same as the extensive awareness
It is aware I am That.

What is left

When the identities and whereabouts are excluded of all
possible components and compositions, of the 'Who' which is
asking what the witness is aware of, the only certain
conclusion is the Who is That which is everything.

Alternatively, by the love of relentless devotion, continuous
effort of persevering is rewarded with realising devotion is
none other than the Self which is That which is everything.

What does not change

We get to I am the witness, then to I am awareness.
We arrive at I am That, then to I am the awareness of That
which is common to everything, which still exists even when
our form has gone.

The universe began and has changed, planets, stars and
galaxies come and go as our form will also. We have only one
thing in common, awareness.

Who is asking

When after a moment or years of asking 'Who am I'
'Who' is asking is asked without an I,
Awareness of existence only is what remains
And we realise our awareness of being is part of All awareness.

The Self is the witness

Asking 'Who am I' with extinction of the I is the Self.
The witness exists as unified thought-free awareness in serene
stillness.

Resignation

My thinking tried so many times it became exhausted.
Eventually in continual exhaustion, I saw what I was trying to
do was impossible and the only thing left was resignation.

I resigned to being whatever was left of me but after all the
asking Who am I, what was left was awareness of I Am-ness.

Cycles of transcendence

Inspired by one person's original transcendental state, organised religions originated to show how to experience this state but not teaching how to experience the state which created them, they outlived their meaning.

Searching to be shown how to experience transcendence, we can easily trust someone with the most advertising and promotion, rather than ourselves, a presence or a picture.

Existence, being and I am are the same

Who am I?
Who is asking?
The witness.

Who is the witness?
The witness is awareness of I am (being or existence)
I am awareness of being.
I am awareness of being That.

Explaining and experiencing

A scientist's method is to explain reality with the tool of
mathematics.
They investigate the forces behind the laws of nature.
Eventually, unable to proceed any further they realise there is
An unfathomable vastly superior intelligent force behind
natures laws.
Which they cannot reach but only accept and resign to.

A mystic's method is to experience reality by the tool of
meditation.
Looking inward they investigate who the Self is
And become aware the Self and everything is one and the same
as an unfathomable vastly superior intelligent force behind
natures laws.
Their experience is awareness of the oneness of reality.

Certainty of Knowing

Asking 'Who am I' is only the beginning because this awareness lets us directly experience 'I am That.' This experience of 'Being That' lets us 'Know I am That.'

We need to remember to just 'Be' That.

We need to remember to guard against falling into the easiest trap of 'thinking' I am That.

We need to not think I am that but 'Be' That, with its certainty of knowing and accompanying bliss.

The searcher

In searching to find our true Self we want to give up our ignorance of what we see as the false Self.

On recognising our true Self the false Self is destroyed as is the search and the searcher.

The end of searching

In our search to lose our ignorance and realise our true Self we realise what we were looking for was in us all along.
Finally, all separateness is lost as nothing has been lost or found only recognised as having been veiled.

We are our problem and solution

In our search for our true Self, thoughts are like clouds veiling what we actually are. Entertaining them Is like accepting mirage water for thirst.

Asking 'Who am I?' shows us true knowledge of the knower and Knowledge being the same. With extinction of the individual I, all that is left is the Self.

Empathic emptiness

At first it can seem as if we cannot understand the person in the film, photograph, drawing, painting or words. It can seem we cannot be aware of their awareness. But eventually, when we put into practise what they suggested, we merge in the only awareness.

2.

Mind

The interior traveller

The mind masquerades as a separate entity the ego. First with a capital i for itself, searching to confirm its existence, but seeing mirage after mirage it cannot say what is truth.

The mind seems over-rational in trying to make sense of its misery but eventually suffering and searching reveals a more subtle and gentle almost feminine presence, a witness in the background, awareness.

Once experienced, awareness may come and go but you know with certainty it is always here, being still in the background, waiting for you to wake up from your delusion.

At first, waking does not last long. Then, awareness of being part of 'all' awareness is experienced, revealing there is no me to be conscious, only awareness of oneness with everything.

Aware

The repetitive loss of concentration every few seconds by the appearance of thoughts shows the persistence of the mind to dominate and veil awareness.

Even though the dominance is unwanted and frequent, the pushing aside of awareness is only temporary. Awareness keeps on returning revealing its gentle presence, each time with increasing significance.

Thoughts relentlessly try to dominate awareness, even when their existence is shown to be imagined, confirming further the reality, awareness always exists, even if veiled.

Desired, with determined patience awareness is unveiled as unimagined and gentle, its permanence in everything is realised as awareness of being.

No reason needed

When we ask 'Who am I' the mind finds first there is a witness then, that the witness is awareness.

But instead of looking for an explanation, a reason for the mind to accept, you can instead just be the answer, be the awareness.

The mind cannot be objective about itself and see itself, but despite this, it can see its limits and accept this limitation.

It is then up to you to accept surrender and resign to awareness's superiority of seeing the mind, and to just be awareness.

Servant of awareness

The ego is compelled to try and prove its existence by continuous production of thought and most of us are stuck with thoughts, putting a damper on our awareness.

If we give up looking for an answer in words.
If we give up trying to reason in words,
We open the door to just being, to awareness.

Staying with awareness, we see the mind is not what we are, but is a product of our awareness and is contained in awareness. The mind is a servant of awareness, and it needs frequent reminding of what it is.

Intangible

When you ask 'Who am I?' ask 'Who' is asking, then you will see you are the subject, trying to witness an object which you cannot because you the subject.

Meditation involves a subject and object but in asking 'Who am I' there is only the subject.

Being aware of the subject is the aim.

Servant

The mind is on a pilgrimage to find the light inside, but on reaching the light the mind recognises its place as servant of the light.

Mind pilgrimage

The mind is on a pilgrimage which can reveal it is a servant of the Self.

The poor old mind needs help because it has been traveling so long without stopping thinking.

It still believes it should stop to think but it could instead consider stopping thinking, then it could see it can just be.

Permanent search

Our way, the way of the mind has not changed in thousands of years. The mind has always tried to find happiness, at first outside then inside.

With loss of happiness the mind finds it has to stay on the path of looking. Even when the mind has found happiness,
It discovers it needs sustenance.

Be stillness

Stillness is awareness of your true Self being fully empty of thoughts.

When experienced, this is knowing and being permanent awareness.

So be still and know you are permanent awareness.

Mirages

The mind like a traveller appears to be on a journey searching for happiness, but just like being in a desert looking for water, it finds mirage after mirage.

The mind thinks when happiness is found the search can end, until it realises happiness cannot be discovered or acquired. Happiness can only be recognised and unveiled inside.

Awareness

Breaking through the cloud of a stream of thoughts, I ask who has broken through and it is the witness. The witness is recognised as always having been here for me, so I know it has not been changed by anything.

Asking the witness what it is, I recognise it as being awareness. It is aware of being, aware of being the same and part of everything.

There is one limitless awareness of existence which is reality.

Imposter

We have an imposter in our midst you and I because we treat each other as separate when we are one.

We are from the same origin, the same earth, the same star and universe. We are the same unseen intangible awareness.

How can you see humanity, or you and I as separate? Would you separate 86 billion brain cells into 86 billion named independent individuals, when they only exist as a human brain because of each other.

When you see me, what you see is the false person. The masks we wear may all look tantalising, beautifully different and interesting, but we all share the same intangible awareness.

Ignoring the mind of thoughts, like a false second person, let us be the unveiled first person, the true Self.

Naming

When we recognise how much we try and name everything,
we realise our mind is trying to make sense of everything
to be important to us and others.

If we try to stop our mind naming people, places, and things,
we become less important and interfering. We leave people
places and things to be what they are.

Our appearance only

More important than the appearance of the person you see in the mirror, their old age, wrinkles and ugliness, is the unaged beauty of the witness aware at them.

3.

What we cannot see

Everything

In our daily struggle to keep our minds free of thoughts, the inner landscape may seem barren like sand, rocks and flint.

But unseen and growing slowly underneath the unremoved veils is the gentle power of awareness, silently showing.

Gently and without effort, for a moment ordinariness is gone, awareness has appeared during the day, changing everything, to Everything.

Just once, then occasionally, then daily, without introduction, inward looking is rewarded with everything as Everything.

How can our natural be permanent?

You

With first glimpses of realisation, your sight is taken and transformed and then given back, but not to you, because you are now not what is just seeing, you are what is being seen in everything you look at.

The presence of what we cannot see

We do not always respect what we cannot see, partly because we think why should we, if there is no evidence it exists. Take respect for love which is trampled on by many but for most is the highest and greatest treasure.

We cannot see how much someone thinks about us, so we cannot see how much they care about us just as they cannot see how much we care about them. We can only show these to each other by being aware.

Turning up and being present, showing in whichever way or form companionship, our unity is expressed through this thing called love, which we cannot see.

We know there are things we cannot see like gravity, sound and radiation. We know they are there because of their effects, but what about effects on us from other things we cannot see?

The presence of what we do not know

How does the Multiverse affect us by it being all space, all time, matter, energy, all other parallel Universes, all consciousness, everything known and unknown? Just because we do not know does not change its effects on us.

On what levels does it interact with us and us with it? Irrespective of time and space are we one and the same by the fact that we all exist, have or will exist?

What does being aware of these possibilities mean? Well, it means we can admit we do not know and have humility. Is this what we understand by fundamental reality, by truth?

Unwise

If we do not know if matter is a particle or a wave form, and
If we do not know if there was a universe before this one,
and if we also do not understand our consciousness or if there
is a multiverse we are part of, we are unwise to state we know
there is no higher consciousness than us.

Recovery

What has been taken from us is not visible to the eye and what we have lost is not visible to the eye. When we realise we have something we cannot see, we realise recognising it is possible.

All we can know

What do we know? We know who we are from the awareness of what we are. How could any animal know anything apart from what it is, which is all we can know.

Knowledge

Awareness of 'I am That' is all I know with certainty.

What we do not know

When we know what we do not know we are not ignorant.

4.

Unifying separateness

The capital of capitals

English is the only language to capitalise the 'i' encouraging individualism and separation from others.

Grief

Grief is unique to each of us and lasts because love and loss cannot exist without each other.

There is nothing to work through grief for except to stay with the grief of loss and love, to be true to it and it will be true to you.

Conversations let the reason we loved continue uninterrupted by their death.

The only separation is of the body as there is no separation of what is one.

The intangible

There is the pain and suffering of loss in grief which only come from love which we think, imagine and then believe has gone.

But where could it have gone? It is here now as it was before. Between then and now, how could our love have changed.

Although intangible, our love does not change. The only change is the object we projected it on to, which like our love, now also can not be seen, but our love is still here.

Because we cannot see it why should it change or go. We only 'seem' to change because we become more aware of it and more aware of our own intangibility, which does not change.

.

Love and loss

The loss of someone you love can be like finding yourself in a powerful river where you have no control and no words.

All you can do is keep afloat, so you can breathe until the river and you become one with the ocean.

Earthrise

The first 'earthrise' photograph from Apollo 8 in 1968 did
not just show swirling white clouds above the blue sea or the
brown landmass.

It showed earth's wholeness with no sign of division into
different nations, races or religions. It showed that we are not
separate but are one.

Maybe everything is held on earth by a gravity of oneness.
Perhaps our unseen witness is kept here and merges with the
unseen witness, the oneness made aware to those in 1968.

Unacceptance of separation

Now is the time because you want something better because
we are in crisis of perpetually being separate. Whatever was
separated in the mythical Garden of Eden, remains as
separation causing painful suffering.

We have our images of the form of whoever took it away.
But why would we try to love whoever took it away? Just to
try and fool them, so we can get our unity back, just to stop our
suffering, not accepting we lost.

Our separation was not taken away frivolously. Either it never
existed as we have not developed that way yet, or most likely,
it was lost because of our confusing love of universal
awareness with the intoxication of worldly greed.

No one said

It is frustrating to find out now after a lot of life has gone that no one ever said, 'This is it.'

They never said 'Right now is it, this very moment of awareness. The existence which we are aware of now is truth and this is it.'

Religion is not essential

Religion's function is to remove our delusion of separateness, to stop seeing ourselves as separate from each other, as independent owners of all that is on this planet. But most religions separate not just us but religion too.

To experience non-religious oneness we have to be together on one planet, as one human race sharing all in peace and in suffering, not separating by having a sense of, i – you - us, from them.

How can we survive like this? Perhaps when there is no alternative and we have to build a bridge to survive, which can only be built when everyone is present and willing.

Being true, this does not show our supposed intelligence as an adaptive tool, fit for purpose, progress, development and attainment, but rather on a lower level of self-destruction.

Perhaps when there are only a few of us left, we will actually be able to listen, hear and speak as one voice, one awareness.

5.

Inside help

In the heart

Who can I turn to now? There seems to be no one of authority to teach and show the way. We can only find the way on our own, so the only way is our way.

Charismatic types seeking new acquisitions or those who say 'I know' are to be avoided. Search inside and you will find the answer is awareness of being still in the heart.

De-hypnotisation

When you ask a teacher to teach you and they say they cannot teach, they are the best teacher.

The best teacher can never teach you. The only function of a teacher is to dehypnotise you to show you how to learn on your own, so that you teach yourself.

Practise

Practise is the best teacher because you become more experienced. A teacher cannot make you more experienced.

The guru

The Guru shows you how to see the veils hiding what you are, but can not remove these veils of ignorance hiding you, as only you can remove the veils.

The Guru does not replace darkness with light as you have to make the effort to turn towards the light.

Who is the guru?

They can be a higher power, a God, a person. They can be alive or dead. They can be an object of worship, a like-minded spiritual group or what is in your heart or head.

Who or whatever the Guru is, they only have one purpose, to show you how to remove the veils of your ignorance of who you think you are, so you recognise your Self, you.

Authority

Who is the authority on authority?
Can there be two or can there be many?
The only true authority is you.

Only the wounded can heal

'Wounded healer, why are you so serious about suffering?
Why do you not break out of healing and be healed?
Is your life only about enduring hardship without complaint?'

'Awareness of being on the path of relief from suffering gives
meaning to suffering. Awareness is reality and cannot be
equalled by anything you see, know, become, acquire or do.'

The wounded place

The wound is where we begin a desire for the happiness we can have inside, from where we begin to be aware of what we are.

Dedication to uncovering our happiness inside by being aware of what we are, gives meaning to our suffering, on the path of happiness.

The wound is where we see others being the same as us, their wound's potential for happiness, from where we access compassion and kindness.

The thread

There is something which seems strange, an occasional small glimmer of warm bright light springing out of our misery and suffering.

It seems to play tricks because it is gone as fast as it came. Not knowing where it came from or went, we dismiss it, then we may miss it until years later.

This time we know it is not playing and is not a stranger. Welcoming it from within from the deepest part of us, it gives us another chance to try again.

It is always present but we do not often uncover it, maybe because distracted, we do not know how to, but the thread of light is here, even now.

No wants

Tangled up, overloaded
In a world of unfairness, misery and suffering,
I look at what my wants are.
They are all happiness, that is all.

What is my relation to the outside world when,
If I do anything, it will have expectations of me.
If I have no wants with no expectations,
The best I can do is, I can be kind.

Expectations

Expectations are beliefs in the future. We are advised not to have them simply because we get attached to them and cling to them emotionally.

Having expectations means we are attached to outcomes and depend on them for our future happiness. We put our happiness in the future. With no expectations we can only be happy now.

It doesnt mean we can't desire happiness. It doesnt mean we can't hope for it in the future. Having hope is acceptance and means letting go of outcomes, so we can be happy now. Hope requires flexibility, humility and letting go of control.

Happiness access

Why must we so often feel a loss of happiness? Loss of happiness is not necessarily sadness. It can be just not being able to access what we know is inside.

6.

Importance

Relevance

Maintaining our peace and happiness requires effort. It involves not being important, not drawing attention by appearing interesting.

Wanting to be irrelevant involves not being interesting. It is being indistinguishable, so as not to be noticed, being ordinary to blend in with the background.

Anyone who has attained inner happiness would not want to risk losing it by describing how to get it, just so they can get applause.

Validation

Do you need validation from others. Do you want to follow the way they reach their conclusion or are you happy certain of you and what you know you are.

The importance of what is not

Do you question if what you need is needed more than what is not.

Do you question if your intelligence is more intelligent than what is not.

Do you question if your health Is healthier than what is not.

Do you question if your beauty is more beautiful than what is not.

Do you question if your relevance is more relevant than what is not.

Do you question if what is important is more important than what is not.

Prelest

If you overindulge in being holy it can make you lose humility, fill you with false pride, appearing deluded or intoxicated and was known as Prelest. Similarly, if you drink too much you become intoxicated and are called drunk.

Perhaps the cure for both is the origins or the other, just as stopping drinking can be achieved by a spiritual path, maybe being too holy with pride and lack of humility can be grounded by senses of the worldly.

Beginning with the end of words

Awareness of realisation begins where words end, when there are no words for i, when words have no importance, when words are redundant, when words cannot communicate.

Until there were words awareness was everything, and so it is again.

Understanding our difficulty

Why do we find it difficult not to speak, not to think about words, not to think in words, not to think, to just be still inside?

Maybe we are over-conditioned to live by other's expectations of us and pass their expectations on.

Always present

When we are ill, or dying, we may not be able to think, move or function normally, but the witness, our awareness, is always present. Whether awake or asleep, the awareness of the witness does not change.

Doctors do not know better

Who says it is this way or that way? What in us wants us to listen to them when we need to go our own way.

Busy just being

Happy appearing not to be doing anything is not idleness.
Happy with just being aware of what we are is the most
attention we can give to anything.

Experience is the only truth

Reading books can show you how something can be done or confirm you did it correctly but is not experience. You cannot learn to sail by reading about a boat's structure or learn about you in books.

Experiential learning can only be about you, done by you. Successes and mistakes and failures are experiential learning.

Tyring again is experiential learning, because repeating experience builds a certainty of knowing. Certainty of experiential knowledge cannot be acquired any other way.

Who you are can not be found in scriptures or books, only inside you.

Remembering Stillness

Because we easily get distracted we have to be reminded.
Because we easily lose focus we have to be reminded.
Because we easily forget we have to be reminded.

Thoughts intrude then sidetrack us from focusing.
Thoughts distract us from our concentration and we forget.
Awareness of stillness returns us.

Our effort

Awareness is always present but accessing it is not automatic. Although it can seem effortless, without sustained effort, awareness is eclipsed by thoughts, so our effort is needed to maintain our awareness.

Now or after another 25 years

You can start at the beginning or the end because it makes no difference, they are the same.

Asking 'Who am I' leads to the question 'Who is the witness' Which leads to the question who or what is the awareness of, then recognising the witness is 'Awareness of I am That.'

Words melt away, displaced and overcome by the experience of being 'Awareness of I am That.'

We do not know

Like everything, something exists or not, but it may not seem to exist yet if it has not been born or made, so time is a factor.

We can only be certain of being aware of I am, as I am here.
We can know we are aware but not that something else is.
We would have to be in its space to know, so space is a factor.

Maybe time and existence are related like awareness and space.

Perhaps our awareness exists beyond time and space and our awareness exists always, everywhere.

Maybe we are entangled as in quantum entanglement.

End of thoughts and stories

When looking at what maintains us suffering in a mundane existence, we know it is our thoughts.

We find words for these thoughts then, spoken or not they become our story to us and others.

Looking to end the effects of thoughts, once the source is found and exposed for what it is, with the story teller gone and no story, there is happiness.

Meaning and attainment

Meaning is the compass guiding us to our goal of staying on the path.

Turbulent thinking

What brought me to here, to here and right now, was a natural reaction to experiencing the unhappiness of turbulent movements of thinking.

Increasingly aware I was becoming more unlike the happiness I knew was inside, I was not willing to go the same way as others.

So, I stayed with where I am, moving less and less until the turbulent movements stopped. I am now more that stillness inside.

Blindness

For a long time I did not know anything. I did not know inner peace and stillness could be discussed. I did not know there are different levels of awareness.

Hearing of these things and unconvinced they were only for others, I took my place of ignorance. I sat, waited and hoped but I was blinded by the blindfold of instructions.

After removing the blindfold of instructions, I decided my own way would be just the question, 'Who is asking?

When our blindness is removed and we are revealed, we see we are awareness of existence, and we each know I am That.

Restoration of sight

I did not know what stillness was until I experienced being
aware of the stillness of no thoughts

Certainty

When you know with certainty 'I am That' there is nothing else to know.

Be Still, ask who and know

Be still and do not be anything else.
Ask who is asking the question being asked.
Know I am That I am.

Concentration and remembering

Concentrating on controlling our mind lets us turn inside. Concentrating on controlling our thoughts lets us stop them and access our stillness.

Remembering to concentrate lets us have more frequent access to our stillness.

Underestimating our potential

Because of our blindness we underestimate our potential,

We underestimate our potential to be wise,

We underestimate our potential to be happy,

We underestimate our potential to realise our true Self,

And it is all reversable by closing our eyes and looking inside.

Everything

Awareness is everything.

Index

Acceptance,	73, 87
All we can know,	64
Always present,	85, 96, 101
Animals,	8, 64
Appearance,	44, 53, 56
Apollo 8,	72
Attainment,	23, 75, 105
Attainment,	
Attainment, Levels of,	23
and Meaning,	105
Attend to the purpose for which	
you have come,	25
Authority,	77, 82
Aware of being,	10, 53
Aware,	44
Awareness,	53, 113
Awareness and consciousness,	6
Be still, ask who and know,	110
Be stillness,	51
Beginning with the end of words,	94
Being and Knowing,	21
Being conscious bliss,	9
(sat-chit-ananda)	
Being the presence of awareness,	5
Blindfold,	107
Blindness,	107, 112
Bliss,	9, 13, 18, 22, 37
Body,	1, 6, 15, 19, 23, 69
Brain,	28, 54
Breath,	71
Busy just being,	98
Capital of capitals,	68
Certainty,	24, 29, 37, 43, 65, 91, 99, 103, 109
Certainty of Knowing,	37
Changing continual to continuous,	27

Charismatic,	77
Clouds,	23, 40, 72
Compass,	105
Compassion,	84
Concentration,	44, 100, 110
Concentration and remembering,	111
Consciousness,	3, 6, 8, 13, 61-62
Continual,	27, 33
Continuous,	27, 29, 46
Cycles of transcendence,	34
Death,	25, 69
De-hypnotisation,	78
Delusion,	12, 43, 75
Desire,	44, 88
Doctors do not know better,	97
Door,	2, 46
Dying,	96
Earthrise,	72
Eclipse,	24
Effort,	11, 16, 23, 25, 29, 80, 90, 101
Effort our most effective weapon,	16
Ego,	14-17, 20, 36, 43, 46
Empathic emptiness,	41
Empty,	22, 51
End of thoughts and stories,	104
Entanglement, quantum,	103
Error,	4
Essence,	8
Everything,	2-3, 7, 9, 131, 17, 28-30, 43-44, 53, 58-59, 61, 72, 94, 98,103, 113
Exclusion,	5
Existence,	4, 8, 15, 19, 23, 31, 35, 43-44, 46, 53, 74, 103-104, 107
Existence, being and I am are the same,	35
Expectations,	86-87, 95
Experience,	4, 7, 18, 21, 23, 34, 36-37, 43, 51, 75, 79, 99, 102, 108
Experience is the only truth,	99

Experiential,	99
Explaining,	36
False,	38, 54
Feminine,	43
Fight,	15, 23
Force, unfathomable behind nature	36
Full,	22, 51
Fully empty,	22, 51
Garden of Eden,	73
Gentle,	23, 44, 58
Glimpses,	11, 17
Gravity,	60, 72
Grief,	69-70
Guru,	80-81
Happiness,	50, 52, 84-85, 88, 90, 104, 106, 112
Happiness access,	88
Healer, The wounded,	83
Heart,	77, 81
Hope,	87
Humility,	61, 93
i,	68
I am aware I am, therefore I think,	4
I am That,	13, 28, 30, 37, 65, 102, 107, 109-110
I Am-ness,	4, 7, 9, 13, 21, 24, 26, 33
Ignorance,	12, 16, 38-39, 80-81, 107
Illusion,	17
Importance,	16, 89, 92, 94
Importance of what is not,	92
Imposter,	54
Inside help,	76
In the heart,	77
Intangible,	47, 54, 70
Intellectual,	3
Intelligent,	8, 92
Interior traveller, The,	43

Intermittent,	11
Interruption,	23
Kindness,	84
Knower,	14, 40
Knowing,	20, 37, 51, 85, 99
Knowledge,	14, 40, 47, 65, 99
Letting go,	24, 87
Levels of attainment,	23
Light,	4, 15-16, 48, 80, 85
Loss,	26, 44, 50, 69-71, 88
Love,	29, 60, 69-71, 73
Love and loss,	69, 71
Masquerading,	16, 43
Mathematics,	36
Meaning,	1, 2, 34, 83-85, 105
Meaning and attainment,	105
Meditation,	36, 47
Method,	7,
Scientist and Mystic	36
Mind,	4, 19-20, 43-46, 48-50, 52, 54-55
Mind pilgrimage,	49
Mirage,	40, 43, 52
Multiverse,	61-62
Mundane existence,	104
Mystic,	36
Name,	20, 54-55
Naming,	54-55
Natural rhythm of Who am I,	18
Nature,	13, 19, 23, 36
Nature and place of the mind, and body,	19
Nature's laws	36
No one said,	74
No reason needed,	45
No wants,	86
Not the I, who I think I am,	1

Now or after another 25 years,   102

Object,   47
Objective,   45
One is part of the other,   15
Oneness,   8, 13, 36, 43, 72, 75
Oneness of being,   13
Only the wounded can heal,   83
Our appearance only,   56
Our effort,   101
Outcome,   87

Pain,   22, 70, 73
Path,   20, 24, 47, 50, 83, 105
Perfection The, of imperfection,   24
Permanent,   1, 4, 23, 50-51, 53
Permanent search,   50
Pilgrimage,   49
Potential,   112
Practise,   41, 79
Prelest,   93
Presence,   5, 34, 43-44, 60-61
Purpose,   22, 25, 75, 81

Quantum Entanglement,   103
Question,   1-2, 92, 102, 107, 110

Realise,   1, 11, 13, 23, 31, 36, 39, 44, 52, 63
Reality,   36, 44, 53, 61, 83
Reason,   45, 46, 69
Reclaiming,   26
Recognise,   18-19, 36, 39, 48, 52-53, 81
Recovery,   63,
Relevance,   90-92
Religion is not essential,   75
Remember,   25, 100, 111
Remembering Stillness,   100
Resignation,   33
Restoration of sight,   108
River,   71

Sat-chit-ananda,	9
(being conscious bliss)	
Scientist,	36
Searcher, The,	38
Searching, The end of,	39
Self and non-Self,	17
Self The, is the witness,	32
Separate,	12, 14, 16, 39, 43, 54, 72-73, 75
Separation, Unacceptance of,	73
Serene,	9, 14-15, 17, 32
Servant,	4, 46, 48-49
Servant of awareness,	46
Sight,	19, 59, 108
Space, time,	61, 103
Spirit,	8, 81, 93
Staring,	22
Stillness,	7, 17, 23, 25, 32, 51, 100,
	106-108, 111
Story,	104
Story teller,	104
Stuff,	8
Subject,	47
Subjective,	6, 21
Suffering,	22, 43, 70, 73, 75, 83-86, 104
Surrender,	45, 47
That,	13, 28-30, 35, 37, 63, 102
The guru,	80
The question,	2
The thread,	85
The intangible,	70
Thinking,	1, 4, 11-12, 28, 33, 36, 49, 106
Thoughts,	1-3, 7, 12, 14-17, 22-23, 25-27,
	31, 36, 48, 44, 46, 50, 53-54,
	58, 100, 104, 108, 111
Time, space,	61, 103
Tools,	36
Transcendent,	6
Transcendence, Cycles of,	34
Truth,	43, 53, 61, 74, 8, 99
Turbulent thinking,	106

Unacceptance of separation,	73
Underestimating our potential,	112
Understanding our difficulty,	95
Unhappy,	2, 112
Unifying separateness,	67
Universe,	3, 8, 30, 53-54, 61-62
Unveil,	10, 16-17, 23, 44, 52, 54
Validation,	90
Veils of ignorance,	12, 80
Veiling,	11, 40
Wants,	86
We are our problem and solution,	40
We do not know,	3, 61-62, 85, 103
What am I?	1
What does not change,	30
What is not,	92
What we cannot see,	60
What we do not know,	62
Who am I,	1-3, 5, 7, 9, 11, 13, 17-18, 23, 28, 31-33, 35-37, 40, 45, 47, 102
Who is asking,	1, 3, 7, 28, 31, 35-36, 107, 110
Who is the guru,	81
Who is the witness?	13, 18, 28, 35, 100
Wise,	112
Without a name,	20
Witness, The,	1, 3-4, 7-10, 13-19, 23, 26, 28-30, 32, 35, 45, 53, 56, 96, 102
Witness, The is the Self,	14
Words,	4, 6-7, 21, 41, 46, 71, 94-95, 102, 104
World,	22, 73, 86, 93
Wound,	83, 84
Wounded place,	84
You,	59

www.ingramcontent.com/pod-product-compliance
Lightning Source LLC
Chambersburg PA
CBHW071551040426

42452CB00008B/1134